AF576950

Recipe:

Serving:

Prep Time:

Cook Time:

Temperature:

Ingredients:

Methods:

Wine Pairing:

From the Kitchen of:

Wine Name

Winery ______ Region ______

Grapes ______ Vintage ______ Alcohol % ______

Appearance		☆ ☆ ☆ ☆ ☆
Aroma		☆ ☆ ☆ ☆ ☆
Body		☆ ☆ ☆ ☆ ☆
Taste		☆ ☆ ☆ ☆ ☆
Finish		☆ ☆ ☆ ☆ ☆

Pairs With	Serving Temperature

Notes

Ratings ☆ ☆ ☆ ☆ ☆

Date ______________ **Caster** ______________

Name of Ritual or Spell ______________

Purpose ______________

Participants **Deities Invoked**

Waxing Full Moon Waning

Description

Ingredients and Equipment

Immediate feelings and effects

Follow Up

Manifestation Date ______________

Results ______________

Recipe: ______________________

Serving: __________ Prep Time: __________

Cook Time: __________ Temperature: __________

Ingredients:

Methods:

Wine Pairing: ______________________

From the Kitchen of: ______________________

Wine Name

Winery ______ Region ______

Grapes ______ Vintage ______ Alcohol % ______

Appearance		☆ ☆ ☆ ☆ ☆
Aroma		☆ ☆ ☆ ☆ ☆
Body		☆ ☆ ☆ ☆ ☆
Taste		☆ ☆ ☆ ☆ ☆
Finish		☆ ☆ ☆ ☆ ☆

Pairs With	Serving Temperature

Notes

Ratings ☆ ☆ ☆ ☆ ☆

Date ____________ **Caster** ____________

Name of Ritual or Spell ____________

Purpose ____________

Participants **Deities Invoked**

Waxing Full Moon Waning

Description

Ingredients and Equipment

Immediate feelings and effects

Follow Up

Manifestation Date ____________

Results ____________

Recipe: ____________________

Serving: __________ Prep Time: __________

Cook Time: __________ Temperature: __________

Ingredients:

Methods:

Wine Pairing: ____________________

From the Kitchen of: ____________________

Wine Name ______________________

Winery ____________ Region ____________

Grapes ____________ Vintage ____________ Alcohol % ________

Appearance		☆ ☆ ☆ ☆ ☆
Aroma		☆ ☆ ☆ ☆ ☆
Body		☆ ☆ ☆ ☆ ☆
Taste		☆ ☆ ☆ ☆ ☆
Finish		☆ ☆ ☆ ☆ ☆

Pairs With	Serving Temperature

Notes

Ratings ☆ ☆ ☆ ☆ ☆

Date ______________ **Caster** ______________

Name of Ritual or Spell ______________

Purpose ______________

Participants **Deities Invoked**

Waxing Full Moon Waning

Description

Ingredients and Equipment

Immediate feelings and effects

Follow Up

Manifestation Date ______________

Results ______________

Recipe: ____________________

Serving: __________ Prep Time: __________

Cook Time: __________ Temperature: __________

Ingredients:

Methods:

Wine Pairing: ____________________

From the Kitchen of: ____________________

Wine Name

Winery

Region

Grapes

Vintage

Alcohol %

Appearance		☆ ☆ ☆ ☆ ☆
Aroma		☆ ☆ ☆ ☆ ☆
Body		☆ ☆ ☆ ☆ ☆
Taste		☆ ☆ ☆ ☆ ☆
Finish		☆ ☆ ☆ ☆ ☆

Pairs With

Serving Temperature

Notes

Ratings ☆ ☆ ☆ ☆ ☆

Date ______________ **Caster** ______________

Name of Ritual or Spell ______________

Purpose ______________

Participants **Deities Invoked**

Waxing Full Moon Waning

Description

Ingredients and Equipment

Immediate feelings and effects

Follow Up

Manifestation Date ______________

Results ______________

Recipe: ____________________

Serving: ____________ Prep Time: ____________

Cook Time: ____________ Temperature: ____________

Ingredients:

Methods:

Wine Pairing: ____________________

From the Kitchen of: ____________________

Wine Name

Winery ______ Region ______

Grapes ______ Vintage ______ Alcohol % ______

Appearance		☆ ☆ ☆ ☆ ☆
Aroma		☆ ☆ ☆ ☆ ☆
Body		☆ ☆ ☆ ☆ ☆
Taste		☆ ☆ ☆ ☆ ☆
Finish		☆ ☆ ☆ ☆ ☆

Pairs With	Serving Temperature

Notes

Ratings ☆ ☆ ☆ ☆ ☆

Date ____________ **Caster** ____________

Name of Ritual or Spell ____________

Purpose ____________

Participants **Deities Invoked**

Waxing Full Moon Waning

Description

Ingredients and Equipment

Immediate feelings and effects

Follow Up

Manifestation Date ____________

Results ____________

Recipe:

Serving:

Prep Time:

Cook Time:

Temperature:

Ingredients:

Methods:

Wine Pairing:

From the Kitchen of:

Wine Name

Winery ______ Region ______

Grapes ______ Vintage ______ Alcohol % ______

Appearance		☆ ☆ ☆ ☆ ☆
Aroma		☆ ☆ ☆ ☆ ☆
Body		☆ ☆ ☆ ☆ ☆
Taste		☆ ☆ ☆ ☆ ☆
Finish		☆ ☆ ☆ ☆ ☆

Pairs With	Serving Temperature

Notes

Ratings ☆ ☆ ☆ ☆ ☆

Date ______________ **Caster** ______________

Name of Ritual or Spell ______________

Purpose ______________

Participants **Deities Invoked**

Waxing Full Moon Waning

Description

Ingredients and Equipment

Immediate feelings and effects

Follow Up

Manifestation Date ______________

Results ______________

Recipe:

Serving:

Prep Time:

Cook Time:

Temperature:

Ingredients:

Methods:

Wine Pairing:

From the Kitchen of:

Wine Name ______________________

Winery ______ Region ______

Grapes ______ Vintage ______ Alcohol % ______

Appearance		☆ ☆ ☆ ☆ ☆
Aroma		☆ ☆ ☆ ☆ ☆
Body		☆ ☆ ☆ ☆ ☆
Taste		☆ ☆ ☆ ☆ ☆
Finish		☆ ☆ ☆ ☆ ☆

Pairs With	Serving Temperature

Notes

Ratings ☆ ☆ ☆ ☆ ☆

Date ____________________ **Caster** ____________________

Name of Ritual or Spell ____________________

Purpose ____________________

Participants **Deities Invoked**

Waxing Full Moon Waning

Description

Ingredients and Equipment

Immediate feelings and effects

Follow Up

Manifestation Date ____________________

Results ____________________

Recipe:

Serving:

Prep Time:

Cook Time:

Temperature:

Ingredients:

Methods:

Wine Pairing:

From the Kitchen of:

Wine Name

Winery

Region

Grapes

Vintage

Alcohol %

Appearance		☆ ☆ ☆ ☆ ☆
Aroma		☆ ☆ ☆ ☆ ☆
Body		☆ ☆ ☆ ☆ ☆
Taste		☆ ☆ ☆ ☆ ☆
Finish		☆ ☆ ☆ ☆ ☆

Pairs With

Serving Temperature

Notes

Ratings ☆ ☆ ☆ ☆ ☆

Date ______________ **Caster** ______________

Name of Ritual or Spell ______________

Purpose ______________

Participants **Deities Invoked**

Waxing Full Moon Waning

Description

Ingredients and Equipment

Immediate feelings and effects

Follow Up

Manifestation Date ______________

Results ______________

Recipe:

Serving:

Prep Time:

Cook Time:

Temperature:

Ingredients:

Methods:

Wine Pairing:

From the Kitchen of:

Wine Name

Winery ______ Region ______

Grapes ______ Vintage ______ Alcohol % ______

Appearance		☆ ☆ ☆ ☆ ☆
Aroma		☆ ☆ ☆ ☆ ☆
Body		☆ ☆ ☆ ☆ ☆
Taste		☆ ☆ ☆ ☆ ☆
Finish		☆ ☆ ☆ ☆ ☆

Pairs With	Serving Temperature

Notes

Ratings ☆ ☆ ☆ ☆ ☆

Date ______________ **Caster** ______________

Name of Ritual or Spell ______________

Purpose ______________

Participants **Deities Invoked**

Waxing Full Moon Waning

Description

Ingredients and Equipment

Immediate feelings and effects

Follow Up

Manifestation Date ______________

Results ______________

Recipe:

Serving:

Prep Time:

Cook Time:

Temperature:

Ingredients:

Methods:

Wine Pairing:

From the Kitchen of:

Wine Name ______________________

Winery ____________ Region ____________

Grapes ____________ Vintage ____________ Alcohol % ________

Appearance		☆ ☆ ☆ ☆ ☆
Aroma		☆ ☆ ☆ ☆ ☆
Body		☆ ☆ ☆ ☆ ☆
Taste		☆ ☆ ☆ ☆ ☆
Finish		☆ ☆ ☆ ☆ ☆

Pairs With	Serving Temperature

Notes

Ratings ☆ ☆ ☆ ☆ ☆

Date ________________ **Caster** ________________

Name of Ritual or Spell ________________

Purpose ________________

Participants

Deities Invoked

Waxing Full Moon Waning

Description

Ingredients and Equipment

Immediate feelings and effects

Follow Up

Manifestation Date ________________

Results ________________

Recipe: ______________________

Serving: ______________ Prep Time: ______________

Cook Time: ______________ Temperature: ______________

Ingredients:

Methods:

Wine Pairing: ______________________

From the Kitchen of: ______________________

Wine Name

Winery _______________ Region _______________

Grapes _______________ Vintage _______________ Alcohol % _______________

Appearance		☆ ☆ ☆ ☆ ☆
Aroma		☆ ☆ ☆ ☆ ☆
Body		☆ ☆ ☆ ☆ ☆
Taste		☆ ☆ ☆ ☆ ☆
Finish		☆ ☆ ☆ ☆ ☆

Pairs With	Serving Temperature

Notes

Ratings ☆ ☆ ☆ ☆ ☆

Date ______________ **Caster** ______________

Name of Ritual or Spell ______________

Purpose ______________

Participants **Deities Invoked**

Waxing Full Moon Waning

Description

Ingredients and Equipment

Immediate feelings and effects

Follow Up

Manifestation Date ______________

Results ______________

Recipe:

Serving:

Prep Time:

Cook Time:

Temperature:

Ingredients:

Methods:

Wine Pairing:

From the Kitchen of:

Wine Name ______

Winery ______ Region ______

Grapes ______ Vintage ______ Alcohol % ______

Appearance		☆ ☆ ☆ ☆ ☆
Aroma		☆ ☆ ☆ ☆ ☆
Body		☆ ☆ ☆ ☆ ☆
Taste		☆ ☆ ☆ ☆ ☆
Finish		☆ ☆ ☆ ☆ ☆

Pairs With	Serving Temperature

Notes

Ratings ☆ ☆ ☆ ☆ ☆

Date ____________ **Caster** ____________

Name of Ritual or Spell ____________

Purpose ____________

Participants **Deities Invoked**

Waxing Full Moon Waning

Description

Ingredients and Equipment

Immediate feelings and effects

Follow Up

Manifestation Date ____________

Results ____________

Recipe:

Serving:

Prep Time:

Cook Time:

Temperature:

Ingredients:

Methods:

Wine Pairing:

From the Kitchen of:

Wine Name

Winery ______ Region ______

Grapes ______ Vintage ______ Alcohol % ______

Appearance		☆ ☆ ☆ ☆ ☆
Aroma		☆ ☆ ☆ ☆ ☆
Body		☆ ☆ ☆ ☆ ☆
Taste		☆ ☆ ☆ ☆ ☆
Finish		☆ ☆ ☆ ☆ ☆

Pairs With	Serving Temperature

Notes

Ratings ☆ ☆ ☆ ☆ ☆

Date ______________ **Caster** ______________________

Name of Ritual or Spell ______________________________

Purpose ______________________________________

Participants **Deities Invoked**

Waxing Full Moon Waning

Description

Ingredients and Equipment

Immediate feelings and effects

Follow Up

Manifestation Date ______________________________

Results ______________________________

Recipe: ______________________

Serving: ____________ Prep Time: ____________

Cook Time: ____________ Temperature: ____________

Ingredients:

Methods:

Wine Pairing: ____________________

From the Kitchen of: ____________________

Wine Name ____________________

Winery ____________ Region ____________

Grapes ____________ Vintage ____________ Alcohol % ________

Appearance		☆ ☆ ☆ ☆ ☆
Aroma		☆ ☆ ☆ ☆ ☆
Body		☆ ☆ ☆ ☆ ☆
Taste		☆ ☆ ☆ ☆ ☆
Finish		☆ ☆ ☆ ☆ ☆

Pairs With	Serving Temperature

Notes

Ratings ☆ ☆ ☆ ☆ ☆

Date ______________ **Caster** ______________

Name of Ritual or Spell ______________

Purpose ______________

Participants **Deities Invoked**

Waxing Full Moon Waning

Description

Ingredients and Equipment

Immediate feelings and effects

Follow Up

Manifestation Date ______________

Results ______________

Recipe:

Serving:

Prep Time:

Cook Time:

Temperature:

Ingredients:

Methods:

Wine Pairing:

From the Kitchen of:

Wine Name ____________________

Winery __________ Region __________

Grapes __________ Vintage __________ Alcohol % ______

Appearance		☆ ☆ ☆ ☆ ☆
Aroma		☆ ☆ ☆ ☆ ☆
Body		☆ ☆ ☆ ☆ ☆
Taste		☆ ☆ ☆ ☆ ☆
Finish		☆ ☆ ☆ ☆ ☆

Pairs With	Serving Temperature

Notes

Ratings ☆ ☆ ☆ ☆ ☆

Date ____________________ **Caster** ____________________

Name of Ritual or Spell ____________________

Purpose ____________________

Participants **Deities Invoked**

Waxing Full Moon Waning

Description

Ingredients and Equipment

Immediate feelings and effects

Follow Up

Manifestation Date ____________________

Results ____________________

Recipe:

Serving:

Prep Time:

Cook Time:

Temperature:

Ingredients:

Methods:

Wine Pairing:

From the Kitchen of:

Wine Name

Winery ______ Region ______

Grapes ______ Vintage ______ Alcohol % ______

Appearance		☆ ☆ ☆ ☆ ☆
Aroma		☆ ☆ ☆ ☆ ☆
Body		☆ ☆ ☆ ☆ ☆
Taste		☆ ☆ ☆ ☆ ☆
Finish		☆ ☆ ☆ ☆ ☆

Pairs With	Serving Temperature

Notes

Ratings ☆ ☆ ☆ ☆ ☆

Date ______________ **Caster** ______________

Name of Ritual or Spell ______________

Purpose ______________

Participants **Deities Invoked**

Waxing Full Moon Waning

Description

Ingredients and Equipment

Immediate feelings and effects

Follow Up

Manifestation Date ______________

Results ______________

Recipe: ______________________________

Serving: ____________ Prep Time: ____________

Cook Time: ____________ Temperature: ____________

Ingredients:

Methods:

Wine Pairing: ____________________

From the Kitchen of: ____________________

Wine Name

Winery ______ Region ______

Grapes ______ Vintage ______ Alcohol % ______

Appearance		☆ ☆ ☆ ☆ ☆
Aroma		☆ ☆ ☆ ☆ ☆
Body		☆ ☆ ☆ ☆ ☆
Taste		☆ ☆ ☆ ☆ ☆
Finish		☆ ☆ ☆ ☆ ☆

Pairs With	Serving Temperature

Notes

Ratings ☆ ☆ ☆ ☆ ☆

Date ____________ **Caster** ____________

Name of Ritual or Spell ____________

Purpose ____________

Participants **Deities Invoked**

Waxing Full Moon Waning

Description

Ingredients and Equipment

Immediate feelings and effects

Follow Up

Manifestation Date ____________

Results ____________

Recipe:

Serving:

Prep Time:

Cook Time:

Temperature:

Ingredients:

Methods:

Wine Pairing:

From the Kitchen of:

Wine Name ______________________

Winery ____________ Region ____________

Grapes ____________ Vintage ____________ Alcohol % ________

Appearance		☆ ☆ ☆ ☆ ☆
Aroma		☆ ☆ ☆ ☆ ☆
Body		☆ ☆ ☆ ☆ ☆
Taste		☆ ☆ ☆ ☆ ☆
Finish		☆ ☆ ☆ ☆ ☆

Pairs With	Serving Temperature

Notes

Ratings ☆ ☆ ☆ ☆ ☆

Date ____________ **Caster** ____________

Name of Ritual or Spell ____________

Purpose ____________

Participants **Deities Invoked**

Waxing Full Moon Waning

Description

Ingredients and Equipment

Immediate feelings and effects

Follow Up

Manifestation Date ____________

Results ____________

Recipe:

Serving:

Prep Time:

Cook Time:

Temperature:

Ingredients:

Methods:

Wine Pairing:

From the Kitchen of:

Wine Name

Winery

Region

Grapes

Vintage

Alcohol %

Appearance		☆ ☆ ☆ ☆ ☆
Aroma		☆ ☆ ☆ ☆ ☆
Body		☆ ☆ ☆ ☆ ☆
Taste		☆ ☆ ☆ ☆ ☆
Finish		☆ ☆ ☆ ☆ ☆

Pairs With

Serving Temperature

Notes

Ratings ☆ ☆ ☆ ☆ ☆

Date ____________ **Caster** ____________

Name of Ritual or Spell ____________

Purpose ____________

Participants **Deities Invoked**

Waxing Full Moon Waning

Description

Ingredients and Equipment

Immediate feelings and effects

Follow Up

Manifestation Date ____________

Results ____________

Recipe:

Serving:

Prep Time:

Cook Time:

Temperature:

Ingredients:

Methods:

Wine Pairing:

From the Kitchen of:

Wine Name ______________________

Winery ____________ Region ____________

Grapes ____________ Vintage ____________ Alcohol % ________

Appearance		☆ ☆ ☆ ☆ ☆
Aroma		☆ ☆ ☆ ☆ ☆
Body		☆ ☆ ☆ ☆ ☆
Taste		☆ ☆ ☆ ☆ ☆
Finish		☆ ☆ ☆ ☆ ☆

Pairs With	Serving Temperature

Notes

Ratings ☆ ☆ ☆ ☆ ☆

Date ______________ **Caster** ______________

Name of Ritual or Spell ______________

Purpose ______________

Participants **Deities Invoked**

Waxing Full Moon Waning

Description

Ingredients and Equipment

Immediate feelings and effects

Follow Up

Manifestation Date ______________

Results ______________

Recipe:

Serving:

Prep Time:

Cook Time:

Temperature:

Ingredients:

Methods:

Wine Pairing:

From the Kitchen of:

Wine Name

Winery ______ Region ______

Grapes ______ Vintage ______ Alcohol % ______

Appearance		☆ ☆ ☆ ☆ ☆
Aroma		☆ ☆ ☆ ☆ ☆
Body		☆ ☆ ☆ ☆ ☆
Taste		☆ ☆ ☆ ☆ ☆
Finish		☆ ☆ ☆ ☆ ☆

Pairs With	Serving Temperature

Notes

Ratings ☆ ☆ ☆ ☆ ☆

Date ______________ **Caster** ______________________

Name of Ritual or Spell ______________________________

Purpose ______________________________________

Participants **Deities Invoked**

Waxing Full Moon Waning

Description

Ingredients and Equipment

Immediate feelings and effects

Follow Up

Manifestation Date ______________________________

Results ______________________________

Recipe:

Serving:

Prep Time:

Cook Time:

Temperature:

Ingredients:

Methods:

Wine Pairing:

From the Kitchen of:

Wine Name ____________________

Winery ______________ Region ______________

Grapes ______________ Vintage ______________ Alcohol % ________

Appearance		☆ ☆ ☆ ☆ ☆
Aroma		☆ ☆ ☆ ☆ ☆
Body		☆ ☆ ☆ ☆ ☆
Taste		☆ ☆ ☆ ☆ ☆
Finish		☆ ☆ ☆ ☆ ☆

Pairs With	Serving Temperature

Notes

Ratings ☆ ☆ ☆ ☆ ☆

Date ____________ **Caster** ____________

Name of Ritual or Spell ____________

Purpose ____________

Participants **Deities Invoked**

Waxing Full Moon Waning

Description

Ingredients and Equipment

Immediate feelings and effects

Follow Up

Manifestation Date ____________

Results ____________

Recipe: ______________________

Serving: __________ Prep Time: __________

Cook Time: __________ Temperature: __________

Ingredients:

Methods:

Wine Pairing: ______________________

From the Kitchen of: ______________________

Wine Name ______________________

Winery ______________ Region ______________

Grapes ______________ Vintage ______________ Alcohol % ________

Appearance		☆ ☆ ☆ ☆ ☆
Aroma		☆ ☆ ☆ ☆ ☆
Body		☆ ☆ ☆ ☆ ☆
Taste		☆ ☆ ☆ ☆ ☆
Finish		☆ ☆ ☆ ☆ ☆

Pairs With	Serving Temperature

Notes

Ratings ☆ ☆ ☆ ☆ ☆

Date ____________ **Caster** ____________

Name of Ritual or Spell ____________

Purpose ____________

Participants **Deities Invoked**

Waxing Full Moon Waning

Description

Ingredients and Equipment

Immediate feelings and effects

Follow Up

Manifestation Date ____________

Results ____________

Recipe: ______________________

Serving: __________ Prep Time: __________

Cook Time: __________ Temperature: __________

Ingredients:

Methods:

Wine Pairing: ______________________

From the Kitchen of: ______________________

Wine Name ______________________

Winery ______________ Region ______________

Grapes ______________ Vintage ______________ Alcohol % __________

Appearance		☆ ☆ ☆ ☆ ☆
Aroma		☆ ☆ ☆ ☆ ☆
Body		☆ ☆ ☆ ☆ ☆
Taste		☆ ☆ ☆ ☆ ☆
Finish		☆ ☆ ☆ ☆ ☆

Pairs With	Serving Temperature

Notes

Ratings ☆ ☆ ☆ ☆ ☆

Date ______________ **Caster** ______________

Name of Ritual or Spell ______________

Purpose ______________

Participants **Deities Invoked**

Waxing Full Moon Waning

Description

Ingredients and Equipment

Immediate feelings and effects

Follow Up

Manifestation Date ______________

Results ______________

Recipe: ____________________

Serving: __________ Prep Time: __________

Cook Time: __________ Temperature: __________

Ingredients:

Methods:

Wine Pairing: ____________________

From the Kitchen of: ____________________

Wine Name ____________________

Winery ____________ Region ____________

Grapes ____________ Vintage ____________ Alcohol % ________

Appearance		☆ ☆ ☆ ☆ ☆
Aroma		☆ ☆ ☆ ☆ ☆
Body		☆ ☆ ☆ ☆ ☆
Taste		☆ ☆ ☆ ☆ ☆
Finish		☆ ☆ ☆ ☆ ☆

Pairs With	Serving Temperature

Notes

Ratings ☆ ☆ ☆ ☆ ☆

Date ______________ **Caster** ______________

Name of Ritual or Spell ______________

Purpose ______________

Participants **Deities Invoked**

Waxing Full Moon Waning

Description

Ingredients and Equipment

Immediate feelings and effects

Follow Up

Manifestation Date ______________

Results ______________

Recipe:

Serving: Prep Time:

Cook Time: Temperature:

Ingredients: Methods:

Wine Pairing:

From the Kitchen of:

Wine Name

Winery | Region

Grapes | Vintage | Alcohol %

Appearance		☆ ☆ ☆ ☆ ☆
Aroma		☆ ☆ ☆ ☆ ☆
Body		☆ ☆ ☆ ☆ ☆
Taste		☆ ☆ ☆ ☆ ☆
Finish		☆ ☆ ☆ ☆ ☆

Pairs With	Serving Temperature

Notes

Ratings ☆ ☆ ☆ ☆ ☆

Date ________________ **Caster** ________________

Name of Ritual or Spell ________________

Purpose ________________

Participants **Deities Invoked**

Waxing Full Moon Waning

Description

Ingredients and Equipment

Immediate feelings and effects

Follow Up

Manifestation Date ________________

Results ________________

Recipe:

Serving:

Prep Time:

Cook Time:

Temperature:

Ingredients:

Methods:

Wine Pairing:

From the Kitchen of:

Wine Name

Winery ______ Region ______

Grapes ______ Vintage ______ Alcohol % ______

Appearance		☆ ☆ ☆ ☆ ☆
Aroma		☆ ☆ ☆ ☆ ☆
Body		☆ ☆ ☆ ☆ ☆
Taste		☆ ☆ ☆ ☆ ☆
Finish		☆ ☆ ☆ ☆ ☆

Pairs With	Serving Temperature

Notes

Ratings ☆ ☆ ☆ ☆ ☆

Date ____________ **Caster** ____________

Name of Ritual or Spell ____________

Purpose ____________

Participants **Deities Invoked**

Waxing Full Moon Waning

Description

Ingredients and Equipment

Immediate feelings and effects

Follow Up

Manifestation Date ____________

Results ____________

Recipe: ______________________

Serving: ____________ Prep Time: ____________

Cook Time: ____________ Temperature: ____________

Ingredients:

Methods:

Wine Pairing: ______________________

From the Kitchen of: ______________________

Wine Name

Winery ______ Region ______

Grapes ______ Vintage ______ Alcohol % ______

Appearance		☆ ☆ ☆ ☆ ☆
Aroma		☆ ☆ ☆ ☆ ☆
Body		☆ ☆ ☆ ☆ ☆
Taste		☆ ☆ ☆ ☆ ☆
Finish		☆ ☆ ☆ ☆ ☆

Pairs With	Serving Temperature

Notes

Ratings ☆ ☆ ☆ ☆ ☆

Date ____________________ **Caster** ______________________________

Name of Ritual or Spell ______________________________

Purpose ______________________________

Participants **Deities Invoked**

Waxing			Full Moon			Waning
●	◐	◑	○	◐	◑	●

Description

Ingredients and Equipment

Immediate feelings and effects

Follow Up

Manifestation Date ______________________________

Results ______________________________

Recipe:

Serving:

Prep Time:

Cook Time:

Temperature:

Ingredients:

Methods:

Wine Pairing:

From the Kitchen of:

Wine Name

Winery ____________ Region ____________

Grapes ____________ Vintage ____________ Alcohol % ____________

Appearance		☆ ☆ ☆ ☆ ☆
Aroma		☆ ☆ ☆ ☆ ☆
Body		☆ ☆ ☆ ☆ ☆
Taste		☆ ☆ ☆ ☆ ☆
Finish		☆ ☆ ☆ ☆ ☆

Pairs With	Serving Temperature

Notes

Ratings ☆ ☆ ☆ ☆ ☆

Date ______________ **Caster** ______________

Name of Ritual or Spell ______________

Purpose ______________

Participants **Deities Invoked**

Waxing Full Moon Waning

Description

Ingredients and Equipment

Immediate feelings and effects

Follow Up

Manifestation Date ______________

Results ______________

Recipe:

Serving:

Prep Time:

Cook Time:

Temperature:

Ingredients:

Methods:

Wine Pairing:

From the Kitchen of:

Wine Name ______________________

Winery ______________ Region ______________

Grapes ______________ Vintage ______________ Alcohol % __________

Appearance		☆ ☆ ☆ ☆ ☆
Aroma		☆ ☆ ☆ ☆ ☆
Body		☆ ☆ ☆ ☆ ☆
Taste		☆ ☆ ☆ ☆ ☆
Finish		☆ ☆ ☆ ☆ ☆

Pairs With	Serving Temperature

Notes

Ratings ☆ ☆ ☆ ☆ ☆

Date ______________ **Caster** ______________

Name of Ritual or Spell ______________

Purpose ______________

Participants **Deities Invoked**

Waxing Full Moon Waning

Description

Ingredients and Equipment

Immediate feelings and effects

Follow Up

Manifestation Date ______________

Results ______________

Plant Name **Date Planted**

Water Requirements

Sunlight

☐ Seed ☐ Transplant

Date	Event

Notes

Outcome

Uses

Purchased at: ______________________ Price: ______________

Plant Name **Date Planted**

Water Requirements

Sunlight

☐ Seed ☐ Transplant

Date	Event

Notes

Outcome

Uses

Purchased at: ______________________ Price: ______________

Plant Name	**Date Planted**

Water Requirements 💧 💧💧 💧💧💧   Sunlight ☼ ◐ ●

☐ Seed   ☐ Transplant

Date	Event

Notes

Outcome

Uses

Purchased at: ____________________   Price: ____________

Plant Name	**Date Planted**

Water Requirements (one drop / two drops / three drops)   Sunlight (full sun / partial sun / shade)

☐ Seed   ☐ Transplant

Date	Event

Notes

Outcome

Uses

Purchased at: ____________________   Price: __________

Plant Name	**Date Planted**

Water Requirements 💧 💧💧 💧💧💧 Sunlight

☐ Seed ☐ Transplant

Date	Event

Notes

Outcome

Uses

Purchased at: ______________________ Price: ______________

Plant Name **Date Planted**

Water Requirements

Sunlight

☐ Seed ☐ Transplant

Date	Event

Notes

Outcome

Uses

Purchased at: ____________________ Price: __________

Plant Name	**Date Planted**

Water Requirements 💧 💧💧 💧💧💧 Sunlight

☐ Seed ☐ Transplant

Date	Event

Notes

Outcome

Uses

Purchased at: ______________________ Price: ______________

Plant Name **Date Planted**

Water Requirements

Sunlight

☐ Seed ☐ Transplant

Date	Event

Notes

Outcome

Uses

Purchased at: ____________________ Price: ____________

Plant Name	**Date Planted**

Water Requirements

Sunlight

☐ Seed ☐ Transplant

Date	Event

Notes

Outcome

Uses

Purchased at: ______________________ Price: ____________

Plant Name	**Date Planted**

Water Requirements 💧 💧💧 💧💧💧 Sunlight

☐ Seed ☐ Transplant

Date	Event

Notes

Outcome

Uses

Purchased at: ______________________ Price: ____________

Made in the USA
Middletown, DE
04 December 2019